GUESTS

NAME AND RELATIONSHIP TO PARENTS

_____

_____

ADVICE FOR PARENTS

_____

_____

_____

WISHES FOR BABY

_____

_____

_____

GUESTS

NAME AND RELATIONSHIP TO PARENTS

_____

_____

ADVICE FOR PARENTS

_____

_____

_____

WISHES FOR BABY

_____

_____

_____

GUESTS

NAME AND RELATIONSHIP TO PARENTS

_____

_____

ADVICE FOR PARENTS

_____

_____

WISHES FOR BABY

_____

_____

_____

GUESTS

NAME AND RELATIONSHIP TO PARENTS

_____

_____

ADVICE FOR PARENTS

_____

_____

_____

WISHES FOR BABY

_____

_____

_____

GUESTS

NAME AND RELATIONSHIP TO PARENTS

_____

_____

ADVICE FOR PARENTS

_____

_____

_____

WISHES FOR BABY

_____

_____

_____

GUESTS

NAME AND RELATIONSHIP TO PARENTS

_____

_____

ADVICE FOR PARENTS

_____

_____

_____

WISHES FOR BABY

_____

_____

_____

GUESTS

NAME AND RELATIONSHIP TO PARENTS

_____

_____

ADVICE FOR PARENTS

_____

_____

_____

WISHES FOR BABY

_____

_____

_____

GUESTS

NAME AND RELATIONSHIP TO PARENTS

_____

_____

ADVICE FOR PARENTS

_____

_____

_____

WISHES FOR BABY

_____

_____

_____

GUESTS

NAME AND RELATIONSHIP TO PARENTS

_____

_____

ADVICE FOR PARENTS

_____

_____

_____

WISHES FOR BABY

_____

_____

_____

GUESTS

NAME AND RELATIONSHIP TO PARENTS

_____

_____

ADVICE FOR PARENTS

_____

_____

_____

WISHES FOR BABY

_____

_____

_____

GUESTS

NAME AND RELATIONSHIP TO PARENTS

_____

_____

ADVICE FOR PARENTS

_____

_____

_____

WISHES FOR BABY

_____

_____

_____

GUESTS

NAME AND RELATIONSHIP TO PARENTS

_____

_____

ADVICE FOR PARENTS

_____

_____

_____

WISHES FOR BABY

_____

_____

_____

GUESTS

NAME AND RELATIONSHIP TO PARENTS

_____

_____

ADVICE FOR PARENTS

_____

_____

WISHES FOR BABY

_____

_____

_____

GUESTS

NAME AND RELATIONSHIP TO PARENTS

_____

_____

ADVICE FOR PARENTS

_____

_____

_____

WISHES FOR BABY

_____

_____

_____

GUESTS

NAME AND RELATIONSHIP TO PARENTS

_____

_____

ADVICE FOR PARENTS

_____

_____

WISHES FOR BABY

_____

_____

_____

GUESTS

NAME AND RELATIONSHIP TO PARENTS

_____

_____

ADVICE FOR PARENTS

_____

_____

_____

WISHES FOR BABY

_____

_____

_____

GUESTS

NAME AND RELATIONSHIP TO PARENTS

_____

_____

ADVICE FOR PARENTS

_____

_____

_____

WISHES FOR BABY

_____

_____

_____

GUESTS

NAME AND RELATIONSHIP TO PARENTS

_____

_____

ADVICE FOR PARENTS

_____

_____

_____

WISHES FOR BABY

_____

_____

_____

GUESTS

NAME AND RELATIONSHIP TO PARENTS

_____

_____

ADVICE FOR PARENTS

_____

_____

WISHES FOR BABY

_____

_____

_____

GUESTS

NAME AND RELATIONSHIP TO PARENTS

_____

_____

ADVICE FOR PARENTS

_____

_____

WISHES FOR BABY

_____

_____

_____

GUESTS

NAME AND RELATIONSHIP TO PARENTS

_____

_____

ADVICE FOR PARENTS

_____

_____

WISHES FOR BABY

_____

_____

_____

GUESTS

NAME AND RELATIONSHIP TO PARENTS

_____

_____

ADVICE FOR PARENTS

_____

_____

_____

WISHES FOR BABY

_____

_____

_____

GUESTS

NAME AND RELATIONSHIP TO PARENTS

_____

_____

ADVICE FOR PARENTS

_____

_____

_____

WISHES FOR BABY

_____

_____

_____

GUESTS

NAME AND RELATIONSHIP TO PARENTS

_____

_____

ADVICE FOR PARENTS

_____

_____

_____

WISHES FOR BABY

_____

_____

_____

GUESTS

NAME AND RELATIONSHIP TO PARENTS

_____

_____

ADVICE FOR PARENTS

_____

_____

_____

WISHES FOR BABY

_____

_____

_____

GUESTS

NAME AND RELATIONSHIP TO PARENTS

_____

_____

ADVICE FOR PARENTS

_____

_____

_____

WISHES FOR BABY

_____

_____

_____

GUESTS

NAME AND RELATIONSHIP TO PARENTS

_____

_____

ADVICE FOR PARENTS

_____

_____

_____

WISHES FOR BABY

_____

_____

_____

GUESTS

NAME AND RELATIONSHIP TO PARENTS

_____

_____

ADVICE FOR PARENTS

_____

_____

WISHES FOR BABY

_____

_____

_____

GUESTS

NAME AND RELATIONSHIP TO PARENTS

_____

_____

ADVICE FOR PARENTS

_____

_____

WISHES FOR BABY

_____

_____

GUESTS

NAME AND RELATIONSHIP TO PARENTS

_____

_____

ADVICE FOR PARENTS

_____

_____

_____

WISHES FOR BABY

_____

_____

_____

NAME AND RELATIONSHIP TO PARENTS

_____

_____

ADVICE FOR PARENTS

_____

_____

WISHES FOR BABY

_____

_____

_____

GUESTS

NAME AND RELATIONSHIP TO PARENTS

_____

_____

ADVICE FOR PARENTS

_____

_____

_____

WISHES FOR BABY

_____

_____

_____

GUESTS

NAME AND RELATIONSHIP TO PARENTS

_____

_____

ADVICE FOR PARENTS

_____

_____

_____

WISHES FOR BABY

_____

_____

_____

GUESTS

NAME AND RELATIONSHIP TO PARENTS

_____

_____

ADVICE FOR PARENTS

_____

_____

_____

WISHES FOR BABY

_____

_____

_____

GUESTS

NAME AND RELATIONSHIP TO PARENTS

_____

_____

ADVICE FOR PARENTS

_____

_____

_____

WISHES FOR BABY

_____

_____

_____

GUESTS

NAME AND RELATIONSHIP TO PARENTS

_____

_____

ADVICE FOR PARENTS

_____

_____

_____

WISHES FOR BABY

_____

_____

_____

GUESTS

NAME AND RELATIONSHIP TO PARENTS

_____

_____

ADVICE FOR PARENTS

_____

_____

_____

WISHES FOR BABY

_____

_____

_____

GUESTS

NAME AND RELATIONSHIP TO PARENTS

_____

_____

ADVICE FOR PARENTS

_____

_____

_____

WISHES FOR BABY

_____

_____

_____

NAME AND RELATIONSHIP TO PARENTS

_____

_____

ADVICE FOR PARENTS

_____

_____

_____

WISHES FOR BABY

_____

_____

_____

GUESTS

NAME AND RELATIONSHIP TO PARENTS

_____

_____

ADVICE FOR PARENTS

_____

_____

_____

WISHES FOR BABY

_____

_____

_____

GUESTS

NAME AND RELATIONSHIP TO PARENTS

_____

_____

ADVICE FOR PARENTS

_____

_____

_____

WISHES FOR BABY

_____

_____

_____

GUESTS

NAME AND RELATIONSHIP TO PARENTS

_____

_____

ADVICE FOR PARENTS

_____

_____

_____

WISHES FOR BABY

_____

_____

_____

GUESTS

NAME AND RELATIONSHIP TO PARENTS

_____

_____

ADVICE FOR PARENTS

_____

_____

_____

WISHES FOR BABY

_____

_____

_____

GUESTS

NAME AND RELATIONSHIP TO PARENTS

_____

_____

ADVICE FOR PARENTS

_____

_____

_____

WISHES FOR BABY

_____

_____

_____

GUESTS

NAME AND RELATIONSHIP TO PARENTS

_____

_____

ADVICE FOR PARENTS

_____

_____

_____

WISHES FOR BABY

_____

_____

_____

GUESTS

NAME AND RELATIONSHIP TO PARENTS

_____

_____

ADVICE FOR PARENTS

_____

_____

WISHES FOR BABY

_____

_____

_____

GUESTS

NAME AND RELATIONSHIP TO PARENTS

_____

_____

ADVICE FOR PARENTS

_____

_____

_____

WISHES FOR BABY

_____

_____

_____

GUESTS

NAME AND RELATIONSHIP TO PARENTS

_____

_____

ADVICE FOR PARENTS

_____

_____

_____

WISHES FOR BABY

_____

_____

_____

GUESTS

NAME AND RELATIONSHIP TO PARENTS

_____

_____

ADVICE FOR PARENTS

_____

_____

_____

WISHES FOR BABY

_____

_____

_____

GUESTS

NAME AND RELATIONSHIP TO PARENTS

_____

_____

ADVICE FOR PARENTS

_____

_____

_____

WISHES FOR BABY

_____

_____

_____

GUESTS

NAME AND RELATIONSHIP TO PARENTS

_____

_____

ADVICE FOR PARENTS

_____

_____

_____

WISHES FOR BABY

_____

_____

_____

GUESTS

NAME AND RELATIONSHIP TO PARENTS

_____

_____

ADVICE FOR PARENTS

_____

_____

_____

WISHES FOR BABY

_____

_____

_____

GUESTS

NAME AND RELATIONSHIP TO PARENTS

_____

_____

ADVICE FOR PARENTS

_____

_____

_____

WISHES FOR BABY

_____

_____

_____

GUESTS

NAME AND RELATIONSHIP TO PARENTS

_____

_____

ADVICE FOR PARENTS

_____

_____

_____

WISHES FOR BABY

_____

_____

_____

GUESTS

NAME AND RELATIONSHIP TO PARENTS

_____

_____

ADVICE FOR PARENTS

_____

_____

_____

WISHES FOR BABY

_____

_____

_____

GUESTS

NAME AND RELATIONSHIP TO PARENTS

_____

_____

ADVICE FOR PARENTS

_____

_____

_____

WISHES FOR BABY

_____

_____

_____

GUESTS

NAME AND RELATIONSHIP TO PARENTS

_____

_____

ADVICE FOR PARENTS

_____

_____

_____

WISHES FOR BABY

_____

_____

_____

GUESTS

NAME AND RELATIONSHIP TO PARENTS

_____

_____

ADVICE FOR PARENTS

_____

_____

_____

WISHES FOR BABY

_____

_____

_____

GUESTS

NAME AND RELATIONSHIP TO PARENTS

_____

_____

ADVICE FOR PARENTS

_____

_____

_____

WISHES FOR BABY

_____

_____

_____

GUESTS

NAME AND RELATIONSHIP TO PARENTS

_____

_____

ADVICE FOR PARENTS

_____

_____

_____

WISHES FOR BABY

_____

_____

_____

GUESTS

NAME AND RELATIONSHIP TO PARENTS

_____

_____

ADVICE FOR PARENTS

_____

_____

WISHES FOR BABY

_____

_____

_____

NAME AND RELATIONSHIP TO PARENTS

_____

_____

ADVICE FOR PARENTS

_____

_____

_____

WISHES FOR BABY

_____

_____

_____

GUESTS

NAME AND RELATIONSHIP TO PARENTS

_____

_____

ADVICE FOR PARENTS

_____

_____

WISHES FOR BABY

_____

_____

_____

GUESTS

NAME AND RELATIONSHIP TO PARENTS

_____

_____

ADVICE FOR PARENTS

_____

_____

_____

WISHES FOR BABY

_____

_____

_____

GUESTS

NAME AND RELATIONSHIP TO PARENTS

_____

_____

ADVICE FOR PARENTS

_____

_____

_____

WISHES FOR BABY

_____

_____

_____

GUESTS

NAME AND RELATIONSHIP TO PARENTS

_____

_____

ADVICE FOR PARENTS

_____

_____

_____

WISHES FOR BABY

_____

_____

_____

GUESTS

NAME AND RELATIONSHIP TO PARENTS

_____

_____

ADVICE FOR PARENTS

_____

_____

_____

WISHES FOR BABY

_____

_____

_____

GUESTS

NAME AND RELATIONSHIP TO PARENTS

_____

_____

ADVICE FOR PARENTS

_____

_____

_____

WISHES FOR BABY

_____

_____

_____

GUESTS

NAME AND RELATIONSHIP TO PARENTS

_____

_____

ADVICE FOR PARENTS

_____

_____

WISHES FOR BABY

_____

_____

_____

GUESTS

NAME AND RELATIONSHIP TO PARENTS

_____

_____

ADVICE FOR PARENTS

_____

_____

_____

WISHES FOR BABY

_____

_____

_____

GUESTS

NAME AND RELATIONSHIP TO PARENTS

_____

_____

ADVICE FOR PARENTS

_____

_____

WISHES FOR BABY

_____

_____

_____

GUESTS

NAME AND RELATIONSHIP TO PARENTS

_____

_____

ADVICE FOR PARENTS

_____

_____

_____

WISHES FOR BABY

_____

_____

_____

GUESTS

NAME AND RELATIONSHIP TO PARENTS

_____

_____

ADVICE FOR PARENTS

_____

_____

_____

WISHES FOR BABY

_____

_____

_____

GUESTS

NAME AND RELATIONSHIP TO PARENTS

_____

_____

ADVICE FOR PARENTS

_____

_____

_____

WISHES FOR BABY

_____

_____

_____

GUESTS

NAME AND RELATIONSHIP TO PARENTS

_____

_____

ADVICE FOR PARENTS

_____

_____

_____

WISHES FOR BABY

_____

_____

_____

GUESTS

NAME AND RELATIONSHIP TO PARENTS

_____

_____

ADVICE FOR PARENTS

_____

_____

WISHES FOR BABY

_____

_____

_____

GUESTS

NAME AND RELATIONSHIP TO PARENTS

_____

_____

ADVICE FOR PARENTS

_____

_____

_____

WISHES FOR BABY

_____

_____

_____

GUESTS

NAME AND RELATIONSHIP TO PARENTS

_____

_____

ADVICE FOR PARENTS

_____

_____

_____

WISHES FOR BABY

_____

_____

_____

GUESTS

NAME AND RELATIONSHIP TO PARENTS

_____

_____

ADVICE FOR PARENTS

_____

_____

_____

WISHES FOR BABY

_____

_____

_____

GUESTS

NAME AND RELATIONSHIP TO PARENTS

_____

_____

ADVICE FOR PARENTS

_____

_____

_____

WISHES FOR BABY

_____

_____

_____

GUESTS

NAME AND RELATIONSHIP TO PARENTS

_____

_____

ADVICE FOR PARENTS

_____

_____

_____

WISHES FOR BABY

_____

_____

_____

GUESTS

NAME AND RELATIONSHIP TO PARENTS

_____

_____

ADVICE FOR PARENTS

_____

_____

_____

WISHES FOR BABY

_____

_____

_____

GUESTS

NAME AND RELATIONSHIP TO PARENTS

_____

_____

ADVICE FOR PARENTS

_____

_____

_____

WISHES FOR BABY

_____

_____

_____

GUESTS

NAME AND RELATIONSHIP TO PARENTS

_____

_____

ADVICE FOR PARENTS

_____

_____

_____

WISHES FOR BABY

_____

_____

_____

GUESTS

NAME AND RELATIONSHIP TO PARENTS

_____

_____

ADVICE FOR PARENTS

_____

_____

WISHES FOR BABY

_____

_____

_____

NAME AND RELATIONSHIP TO PARENTS

_____

_____

ADVICE FOR PARENTS

_____

_____

WISHES FOR BABY

_____

_____

_____

GUESTS

NAME AND RELATIONSHIP TO PARENTS

_____

_____

ADVICE FOR PARENTS

_____

_____

WISHES FOR BABY

_____

_____

_____

GUESTS

NAME AND RELATIONSHIP TO PARENTS

_____

_____

ADVICE FOR PARENTS

_____

_____

_____

WISHES FOR BABY

_____

_____

_____

GUESTS

NAME AND RELATIONSHIP TO PARENTS

_____

_____

ADVICE FOR PARENTS

_____

_____

_____

WISHES FOR BABY

_____

_____

_____

Attach Keepsakes and Pictures

★ GIFT LOG ★

★ GIFT LOG ★

GIFT RECEIVED	GIVEN BY

★ GIFT LOG ★

GIFT RECEIVED	GIVEN BY

★ GIFT LOG ★

GIFT RECEIVED	GIVEN BY

★ GIFT LOG ★

GIFT RECEIVED	GIVEN BY

★ GIFT LOG ★

GIFT RECEIVED	GIVEN BY

★ GIFT LOG ★

GIFT RECEIVED	GIVEN BY

★ GIFT LOG ★

GIFT RECEIVED	GIVEN BY

★ GIFT LOG ★

GIFT RECEIVED	GIVEN BY

★ GIFT LOG ★

GIFT RECEIVED	GIVEN BY

★ GIFT LOG ★

GIFT RECEIVED	GIVEN BY

Made in the
USA
Monee, IL